ABOUT MENTA ACTUAL

Documents additional progress from someone who was hospitalized due to bipolar mental illness. It is nothing short of a miracle that Mr Medl has written multiple books. What is even more amazing is that he's a mental health advocate who helps other people cope with the same disease. If you don't think mental illness is a real disease, you need to read one or more if Mr Medl's books.

Tom

John has done it again. Another fantastic book in his collection on mental illness. John gets it. John lives it. It's great to get additional insight on bipolar from John in this more recent collection, as well as a few of his interviews where he answered questions about his illness, concerns on mental illness, and police and show they interact with mental illness.

Craig A. Price Jr.

In the mental health community we often feel alone because people don't understand us. After reading through John's book I find a sense of peace. That I wasn't alone and there is hope in recovery. We can't just "get over it" there is a process to healing from the battle we experience in our own head.

Grant Williams

MENTAL ILLNESS IS AN ACTUAL ILLNESS

THOUGHTS, STORIES, AND PHILOSOPHY OF LIFE FROM SOMEONE LIVING WITH MENTAL ILLNESS

WORKINGS OF A BIPOLAR MIND
BOOK 5

JOHN MEDL

Formatted by Craig A. Price Jr.

CONTENTS

1 LOG ENTRY #1

Lots of great things are happening for me. I don't know if my psychiatrist was kidding or not, but he said he wants me to Zoom conference with his other patients just to talk to them. Compared to the other patients at my clinic, I am probably a success story. I don't always feel like a success story, but I'm starting to believe in myself a little more. My high school alma mater, Moeller HS, is going to give me a mention in their Fall Newsletter. I'm working on getting a mention from my college alma mater, The University of Dayton. I am getting shout outs from all over the country regarding my books. I've been making some really great connections to my readers who struggle themselves with mental illness or it runs in their family, or both. It's a little surreal sometimes.

I can't emphasize enough how sick I was when I was first diagnosed with bipolar disorder with psychotic features in 2006. For months, maybe years, (it's foggy), all I could do was eat, sleep, and go to the bathroom. If I took a shower, it was a big accomplishment for the day or week. I was down on the mat several times. Well, I got up every time. That's the only way I know how to be.

2 LOG ENTRY #2

I'M REALLY DOWN ON MYSELF BECAUSE ALL I WANTED TO DO WAS drive to the store, and I can't. I'm exhausted and anxious while driving. I feel so trapped and caged in my house. I love my house, but it would be nice to be able to come and go as I please, instead of it being a big ordeal. I actually have money for once because I have been saving, and I haven't gambled in 39 days or so.

I don't want to be one of those people who need to hear they are doing a good job all the time. My parents and my educational institutions raised me extremely tough, coupled with what I have survived. Of course, it's really nice to hear that people think I am a good person, but I more enjoy when people say they are enjoying my books or my writings. I don't do all this work for money or praise. I do it because there are men and women and their loved one's struggling with this beast called mental illness, and maybe I can bring them some hope and sunshine. Most of the time, I don't even hear much feedback, and I know I am helping people who don't even really know me. I'm just extremely frustrated right now, and it usually helps for me to write about it.

3 LOG ENTRY #3

I HAD A PRETTY COOL IDEA THIS MORNING. I THINK I'M GOING TO start donating books to libraries across the country so that anyone with a library card can read my story. I think I'm going to start with the really big cities first because that will hopefully result in the biggest reach.

I never thought I'd be an author, and furthermore, I never thought my books would be available in the Cincinnati Public Library. That's a pretty big deal to me. When I studied psychology in college, my plans were to go on and get a doctorate/Ph.D. I ran out of money and motivation, so I never accomplished that. I wish The University of Dayton would award me an honorary doctorate like several universities have done for many celebrities, including Bill Cosby, who turned out to be an unsavory character. Maybe I should just go back to school. Anyway, the whole point of this post is to remind people that many of your plans aren't going to work out, but maybe something even better will happen that you never even thought about. It feels good to give up control, and let the universe and the Fates guide your life. Trying to control everything creates a lot of stress, worry, and anxiety.

4 LOG ENTRY #4

This might be long winded, but it's important. I have rarely had to do this, but I called my case manager for help today regarding my mental health. Part of self care is being self aware when I need help. I needed to talk to a professional today. I've had a lot of stress in the last few months, and a lot of major changes. I have been irritable, tired, sore, anxious, manic, and depressed more than usual. I can't stress enough how frustrating and exhausting the rollercoaster ride is. I called for help because I noticed my symptoms were more frequent and more severe than usual. I am asking you all to seek help if you aren't feeling mentally healthy, or even if you just feel a little off. You can always reach out to me at johnmedl7@gmail.com, or call the crisis line (even if you are not suicidal) at 1-800-273-8255 or text HOME to 741741. Don't be ashamed to ask for help, and don't ever let people make you feel like less of a person if you do need help. I am going to try to take it easy for the next few weeks, and I know I will get enjoyment from distributing my books and people visiting.

5 LOG ENTRY #5

THE OTHER DAY, A GUY WAS USING LEAVES FROM A TREE TO WIPE himself and acting strangely. Just now, another guy was walking down the street yelling at cars and every other word was the N word. There's a bus stop near my house, and I can only assume both guys were from the bus stop. I had never seen them in the neighborhood before. I didn't call the cops just now, but I did the other day. I wasn't trying to get anyone in trouble, it's just that it appeared both these guys had mental issues. With my personal and professional experience, it's pretty easy to recognize someone who is mentally unstable. It just makes my heart hurt because I've been there. I also wanted to post about it so that my neighborhood friends on social media know. The first guy didn't seem dangerous, but the guy I just saw was very belligerent and agitated. If these guys are indeed mentally unstable, their behavior could get violent and unpredictable.

6 LOG ENTRY #6

I think most people are just trying to be happy. With their jobs, love interest, financial situation, whatever. All that stuff is just a means to end. That end is happiness. I guess I just don't understand any other way to be. I've chosen to live a simple life. Some of that is out of necessity, and the cards I've been dealt. I practice gratitude frequently. Despite having bipolar depression, I'm happy more often times than not. I like my coffee and cigarette sessions on the porch, music, reading, sports, and a lot of other inexpensive things. Luxury makes me uncomfortable, but some people chase after that stuff. I can't speak for everyone else, but I'm just trying to be happy. I don't understand the point of all this otherwise.

7 LOG ENTRY #7

At the end of the day, I'm the only person who has to live with me the rest of my life. I'm not here to please anyone who doesn't appreciate or understand why I do what I do. I listen to the people I am helping. I listen to their heartbreaking life experiences and fantastic triumphs, and every point in between. We all have unique journeys, mental illness or not. I can't fulfill my purpose if I am constantly living in fear of the "what ifs", and if I don't take care of myself first. I can't help others if I don't allow time for myself. This is one of the biggest things I'm always working on.

It's a little overwhelming, actually. My life wasn't supposed to turn out this way, but here we are. I never dreamed that I would be so satisfied with the work that I do. If you are struggling mentally, please reach out. If not to me, to a loved one, or a trusted friend. We all need help sometimes, and it's okay to not be okay. Much love always.

8 LOG ENTRY #8

> "To know even one life has breathed easier because you have lived. This is to have succeeded."
>
> RALPH WALDO EMERSON

I REALLY BELIEVE IN THIS QUOTE, AND IT HELPS ME THROUGH SOME of my hardest days. Do me a favor, and I know my close friends will do this for me. Don't let me get a big head about all the attention I get with my books and my work. I would consider that a failure to my purpose almost as much as if I gave up. There's a line that some people cross from confidence to arrogance when they think they are special and don't have to play by the rules anymore. I don't want to be like that. I am a humble servant and merely a vessel towards a purpose. I'm still going to enjoy my life and even be selfish sometimes, but it's not all about me.

SELF MEDICATING

I think my self medicating began after the death of my maternal grandmother. I was a sophomore or junior in high school. That would make the year 1998 or 1999. It may have been the first time I had ever felt an immense loss. Shortly after her passing, I took a whiskey bottle in my room and drank most of it. I had a few beers before, but this was the first time I had really gotten drunk. I remember crying while I was drinking the whiskey. I started drinking alcohol more frequently in high school, and I started to smoke marijuana very heavily. The pot smoking began as a sporadic event, but became a several times a day habit. I experimented with harder drugs, but I don't really think my heavier drug use was self medication.

My alcohol and marijuana use continued for well over a decade. I am sober 99% of the time now, but I still get the urge for a beer or two. I was stoned almost every second of every day for a very long time. I drove my car for a living, so I could only drink alcohol when I wasn't working or driving, although sometimes I would drive while intoxicated. I often smoked marijuana while I drove my car around. I don't know why I didn't care about the law. Maybe it's in the invincibility of youth or the grandeur of bipolar disorder.

I was first hospitalized with bipolar disorder with psychotic features in July 2006. I was 24 years old. Before my first hospitalization, no one really thought about the possibility that I may have mental illness. I was in and out of mania and psychosis for a few weeks prior to my hospitalization, but

I wasn't self aware enough or even coherent enough to realize there was something terribly wrong with my behavior.

9 BLOG ENTRY #1

POLICE: HOW I SEE THEM

JOHN MEDL AND JULIE N. STRICKLAND
10/2020

INTRODUCTION (JULIE)

When John Medl offered to guest blog, I jumped at the chance. This website has never been about just Julian. That is, my goal is to help as many people as possible. John has been diagnosed with bipolar disorder and openly advocates for mental health. John was kind enough to write this and answer some follow-up questions, in the hopes of helping others. We are unified in our purpose.

You can read more about John in our previous blog (jnstrickland.com).

ARRESTED (JOHN)

I was arrested during a psychotic episode related to bipolar disorder (No one knew at the time) for trespassing and criminal damaging. I was following coded messages obtained from ordinary objects like lottery tickets and the US Mail to get my reward for uncovering a gang in my neighborhood. I opened the door to an unlocked car and got in the driver's seat. I tried to start the car with a screwdriver. I thought the car was my reward based on these delusional messages I was decoding. I thought I worked for/was helping the CIA, and that there were microphones placed by the government in my house.

I was placed in handcuffs, arrested, and put into the back of the police cruiser. I was non-violent and compliant, even though I was going through mania and psychosis. My conscious mind was gone, and I had no grasp on reality. I was placed in a holding cell with about a dozen other men when we arrived at the police station. Only after I threatened to throw my food tray was I given a phone call and a private cell. I was given a meal of hot dogs, sauerkraut, and white bread. I had to ask for a glass of water. I slept off the mania and psychosis.

I was released in the morning and referred to mental health court as opposed to criminal court. I had an amazing, educated, understanding judge who knew that I needed psychiatric help, and I was not a violent criminal. Because of (now deceased) Judge Stautberg, I have received mostly excellent care since 2006. The verdict in mental health court was not guilty by reason of insanity (NGRI).

I don't really know how much better the police could have handled my situation. I can't recall the officers drawing a weapon of any kind or threatening me. I assume their training told them that I was going to comply, and that I was non-violent, and they were correct. I think I even remember having light, friendly conversation with the officers on the way to the police station. I remember feeling like I was in a taxicab.

I was Caucasian/white, unarmed, friendly, and compliant. I doubt that many mentally unstable people are like this during an arrest. I should also add that I am a man of large stature, both in weight and height, and the police officers still knew I was not a threat. Did their training and education prepare them for a situation like mine? Were they just outstanding police officers? What if they had had a bad day? Would my situation and outcome have been different? The two arresting officers were African American. When you start adding variables to confrontations with the police (weapons, aggression, race, gender, etc.), the danger level rises for everyone involved. The idea is to serve, protect, and preserve life, and at the same time, protect the lives of police officers in deadly/lethal/violent situations. I imagine it's hard to tell the difference between an armed, sane person, and an armed insane person. Is there really a difference to the police officer? A weapon is a weapon, and violence is violence. The police officers have to protect themselves. It's no one's fault when mental health problems are present. It's such a slippery slope.

HOW DO YOU THINK YOUR EXPERIENCE WOULD HAVE BEEN DIFFERENT IF AN AMBULANCE HAD PICKED YOU UP INSTEAD OF THE POLICE?

Going through psychosis like I did is extremely terrifying. I'm not sure if it would have been any less terrifying if an ambulance had picked me up. I remember feeling safe with the police, but again, I had no idea what was going on. I think my experience with the police during psychosis went just about as smoothly as it could have. I know this is not always the case.

SHOULD POLICE BE RESPONSIBLE FOR PICKING UP PEOPLE WHO ARE EXPERIENCING PSYCHOSIS?

Only if they are breaking the law. Police officers' primary job is to enforce the law. If someone going through psychosis is not breaking the law, let's hope that person gets help on their own or has family members that will help him/her. I will say that I think there is an exception where if the person going through psychosis is demonstrating odd or dangerous behavior, then yes, I think it's up to the police to direct that person to the proper resources. This means that police officers need to be trained about mental illness and psychosis. I remember in my psychology classes watching plenty of videos of people with mental illness. Videos like those would help officers identify a nonviolent, mentally unstable person versus someone breaking the law out of his/her own choice.

WOULD HAVING A SOCIAL WORKER PRESENT HELP?

I'm not really sure. You are adding another life to the dangerous situation. I think social workers are trained well enough to handle people during psychosis, but I don't know how the logistics would play out. Would a social worker ride along with the police on every run? It just doesn't seem like it would work out. You might have a situation where a case worker is present during an armed robbery, for example. That doesn't seem very helpful or safe.

When I was hospitalized during mania and psychosis, I was given a very heavy sedative via syringe. I remember being terrified and surrounded by police officers and security guards. I think I remember about a dozen officers, all armed. It's a little blurry. I have no idea how I finally gave in and let the nurse administer the shot. Even in my psychosis, I think I realized I was outnumbered.

ALAN PEAN WAS SHOT WHILE AT A HOSPITAL IN HOUSTON, WHERE HE HAD CHECKED HIMSELF IN. WHAT ARE YOUR THOUGHTS WHEN READING ABOUT HIS EXPERIENCE?

https://www.nytimes.com/2016/02/14/us/hospital-guns-mental-health.html

I think there was definitely a mishandling in the case of Alan Pean. He could have been restrained more peacefully than being shot. Then, he could have received proper psychiatric care, which would probably include a sedative followed by close monitoring or a hospital stay. He showed all the signs of mental instability, and even stated so on several occasions. It was amazing that Alan Pean was self-aware enough to state that he was manic. If someone going through mania and psychosis knows what's going on, the police officers should have listened and taken less violent steps, as I stated previously.

SUMMARY (JULIE)

You are important. You matter.

Email: jules2620@gmail.com
IG: @julie.n.strickland
FB: The Walls Are Breathing (jnstrickland)
Twitter: @JulieNStrick
Website: jnstrickland.com
#CureStigma #NoStigma

10 LOG ENTRY #9

I don't remember much from my days on the couch after I was first released from the hospital. Almost 15 years ago now. All I could do was eat, sleep, and go to the bathroom. My mom would set out a towel and my clothes about once a week for me to take a shower. I took a shower last night. It felt great, and it wasn't really difficult like it used to be. I used to get dizzy and claustrophobic in the shower. It had been a few days.

Personal hygiene is often difficult for people with mental illness. Experts think it's because having a mental illness is just so exhausting that tasks like showering are just too much energy to exert. I can't remember too many visitors in those days on the couch. I can't even tell you how long I was confined to the couch. My mom tells me that she remembers the first joke I made after being released from the hospital. I vaguely remember that, too.

My parents, as much as any doctor, deserve credit for

nursing me back to health. This is why and how I can say that I'm blessed. I remember those dark days. I remember those days in my worst days in the present. I don't know how I fought through it, to be honest. Maybe I was just sedated into indifference. When I tell people that I feel blessed, most don't understand how I can say that. Mental illness can be a blessing in disguise sometimes, but in general, it's a severe hindrance. There are all sorts of ranges of severity, but usually it's a major life obstacle. Often times, it is so severe that mental illness is labeled a disability, which is the case for me. Disability does not mean inability. I can do many things well, but I am not well enough to hold down a job or manage my own finances. Some days, I am still very symptomatic.

I just don't know any other way to be. From the way I was raised to my life experiences to all the people who have crossed my path. I'm extremely proud of myself for never giving up and the work that I do. When I help others, it helps me heal too.

11 LOG ENTRY #10

Positive thinking does not come naturally to a lot of us with anxiety and depression. There are times when I can't manage a single positive thought. However, I have been practicing positivity for a long time, like any craft, and I have gotten pretty good at it. But I had to practice. It started with me reading inspirational and motivational quotes. I had to stop watching most TV and the news. I have to take breaks from social media. I am sober almost always. I am 100% medicine compliant.

All of these things that I cut out of my life were feeding my anxiety and depression, like gasoline. I still drink a lot of coffee, which is terrible for my anxiety, but I'm between a rock and a hard place. I take sedatives to keep me calm, which in turn, makes me drowsy and tired. I want to be awake and lively, so I drink coffee to wake myself up. I get hyper only to be sedated again. This is called the vicious cycle of anxiety.

The point I want to make is that you have no chance

surviving anxiety and depression if you feed it with triggers. Cut out as many triggers as you can so you have a fighting chance. Then, you can replace the triggers with positivity, gratitude, music, journaling, gardening, whatever gives you relief in a healthy way.

12 LOG ENTRY #11

Mental illness is a deceptive term because it implies that symptoms are only present "in our heads". Of course, mental illness is literally in our heads because that's where our brains are. On average, a person with bipolar disorder lives 9 years less than the average healthy person. Think about what kind of mental and physical trauma "mental illness" can do to the body to cause 9 whole years to be taken from someone's life. Some recurring physical symptoms I have are: stiff joints, chest pains, sweating, itching, and I can't sit still sometimes. These are just a few. Yes, I have mental symptoms like brain fog, repeating/negative thoughts, paranoia, and I've experienced psychosis, which is a total break from reality several times. I just want to point out that mental illness is not just a mental illness, if that makes sense.

13 LOG ENTRY #12

I'M FEELING A LITTLE EXTRA BLESSED TODAY. I HAD TO HAVE A major truck repair, and I went without a car for almost two weeks. My truck is fixed now, and I drove myself, unmedicated, to the gas station. It was so nice. I am going to try to work on my driving skills so I can get out of my house more. I've gone 74 days now without gambling even a penny, so I actually have a little money in my pocket. I was able to read a few chapters in the book I'm reading for the first time in months. My symptoms have been fairly calm today, and I don't have to do any major work until I get my next shipment of books in about two weeks. I'm going to try to help around the house a little more and maybe cook dinner a night or two. My birthday is on October 22nd, and I'm looking forward to celebrating with a few friends and my family. Birthdays are a big deal to me ever since I got sick because I feel so lucky to still be alive. I thought I was a goner so many times. I also feel like it's a middle finger to my illness when I survive another year.

14 LOG ENTRY #13

It's a weird feeling to think that so many people are interested in my writings. Writing is second nature to me and also a coping mechanism for my illness, so it's almost like if people wanted to watch me breathe. I thought by now I would be a millionaire doing what millionaires do. Maybe real estate or something. I chased that dream for a long time, then one day, I realized I didn't want that lifestyle. I was literally killing myself, physically and mentally, to try to outdo other people and acquire wealth. I thought the whole point in life was to become rich.

Then I started doing advocacy work and writing books. It's more rewarding than I ever thought any career could be. I'm just not money motivated anymore. I'm not willing to risk my health and happiness for it. I guess I thought I couldn't be happy without a lot of money.

15 POEM ENTRY #1

I'm a dimly lit candle
Among the fires burning inside me.
I'm my biggest hero and harshest critic.
I commiserate with the sick
And plead to the cynics.
Everyone has made up their minds.
And I'm just an hourglass
Waiting for the sands of time.

16 LOG ENTRY #14

I HAD AN ENGLISH TEACHER IN HIGH SCHOOL NAMED MS. Phoebus. She used to call me Johnny Swagger. I always liked the nickname, although people usually just call me Medl, even to this day. I guess I could be cocky at times in high school. I have no idea what I had to be so cocky about. Looking back, I was such a fool, at least to compared to how much I have learned since then. I believe I'm a good person and a talented writer and many other great qualities, but I still lack confidence. Sometimes I wonder if this is why I have social anxiety sometimes, even around my closest of friends. My hunch is that is another chemical failure in my brain. I am looking for a more quiet confidence now, and I have to work on that. Some days, I think I want my high school swagger back, but then I remember how young and foolish I was. I guess I am looking for a confidence level somewhere between outrageously cocky and a nervous wreck.

17 LOG ENTRY #15

When I say that I'm blessed, I don't necessarily mean that in a religious way, although it doesn't bother me if someone interprets it that way. I mean it in a superlative way. I think the word blessed is just as about as complimentary as I can get with my life. Charmed is a little too dramatic for me, but it's the same idea. A lot of people, after hearing my story, don't understand how I can say that I'm blessed. First of all, I'm alive, which is amazing in itself, and secondly, I have everything I need. I also get to write and advocate for the sick for a living. It's very rewarding work. That's just how I feel about my life.

I want to show people that someone can have a mental illness and not be crazy, in the generic sense of the word. I actually hate that word and label, and I try to avoid using it whenever I can. My brain is sick, just like a person who has cancer or diabetes. I take medication for it. Most of the time, the pills work. Sometimes, the medication is not enough, and I have to rely on coping skills and experience. I'm not comparing hardships, but I'm trying to point out that mental illness is still an illness, even though it is mostly invisible. My symptoms can be very visible, and only my close friends and family have seen me symptomatic. Aside from professionals, of course.

18 LOG ENTRY #16

THINGS I FIND ANNOYING

1. Infatuation with politics and politicians. Do you really think most of them give a damn about common people? Some people act like politicians are their friends or family or something. Super annoying.
2. Most people don't think that people on disability or food assistance deserve it. A lot of people think it's some kind of free ride where everyone is living the high life on $38 a month (that's what I get in food stamps). It also took me 7 years to get approved for disability. The government doesn't just hand it out like free samples at the grocery.
3. Most people have no clue how painful mental illness is. Physically, mentally, emotionally, etc. I try to

educate people the best I can, but only so many people read my books or social media posts. Only my parents see me curled up in bed in pain on a fairly regular basis. I don't talk about my struggles as much as my victories because I don't want sympathy. Save that for the hungry and homeless who are going to be sleeping outside this Winter.

19 LOG ENTRY #17

I HAD A LITTLE ROUGH PATCH TONIGHT. NOTHING TERRIBLE. Anxiety and mania. I always tell myself, "it wasn't that bad". But it is. It's hard for me to remember life and how I felt before symptoms and medication. And I know this sounds irrational, but I don't know if I would want to be cured if there was one. I've gained so much.

20 POEM ENTRY #2

11-4-2020

When the blissful moments
Are fleeting, hold on
With everything you have.
These are the moments
That make up our best memories.
Maybe the afterlife is just
Reliving precious moments over
And over again.
Or maybe we'll get another chance
To spin the wheel again
To correct the wrongs of the evil
And maybe good will prevails next time.

21 LOG ENTRY #18

KINDNESS HELPS ME MAKE SENSE OF LIFE. I WOULD LIKE TO THINK I've always been kind, but my desire to be kind has gotten stronger since I have been ill. I think I like the way kindness makes me feel, and in a way, I'm just giving back to the universe for all the kindness I have been shown. Maybe I like the way my kindness makes others feel. It definitely benefits me in a therapeutic way.

22 LOG ENTRY #19

When I have a negative emotion or adverse reaction to something, I wonder if my emotions fall into the range of a normal, prudent person (because of my illness). I dislike the term normal, but I am only using it here to differentiate from abnormal. I think feelings and reactions are always on a spectrum. I could have irritability or anxiety or intense sadness, and many other emotions that come along with having mental illness. Am I being irrotational? Are my feelings still valid even though they are fueled by an abnormal brain? I think my feelings are valid even when I am being irrational because those are the emotions I am feeling in reality. Most of the time, an explanation and apology diffuse any tension between myself and other people. When I am very upset, I try to isolate myself so that I do not bring others down into my upset mood. This is not always possible. Being open and honest about my emotions really helps. I think the key is recognizing when I may be irritated or depressed or anxious. When I am self-aware, I can deal with emotional situations in a more reasonable manner. It's frustrating to realize that it's me who is the offender in an emotional situation. I guess everyone wants to be perfect. Maybe I have high standards, or maybe I know, deep down, that I am a kind. loving person. My illness makes me act out of character. I am not my illness. I know this because I act a certain way when I am stable, which is the majority of the time. Since emotional outbursts are sporadic, I know that it is my illness taking over and causing me to act in a negative way.

23 LOG ENTRY #20

The other day I said to my case manager, "My parents raised a monster". Probably unsettling to hear as a case manager from someone who has had problems with delusions and grandiosity. All I meant is that my parents put high standards on me, and showed by example, never to quit. I've quit things before, but I was referring to my life and recovery. Quitting is not going to happen. It's not an option at all. I've endured some of the most horrible pain that a human can bear. I'm not quitting now when life isn't so bad for me. I didn't endure everything I did to not enjoy the sunshine on the other side.

24 LOG ENTRY #21

MONTH 11 OF THE PANDEMIC YEAR 2020

I'm starting to feel bad for people who aren't used to isolation like I am. Aside from employment issues. I'm just referring to having a social life and traveling and basically "normal" people being able to come and go freely. My anxiety has isolated me for a long time, and it's just weird to see normally functioning people getting a taste of my life. I wouldn't wish it on anyone.

25 LOG ENTRY #22

Time is a weird thing. In my younger years, I would go on weekend long party binges that seemed to only last a few minutes. I felt like I had all the time in the world, and it's up for debate whether it was wasted time. Then, I'd do it all over again the next weekend. Now, I get symptomatic, and minutes and seconds feel like hours. I value time more now, and I think that comes with maturity and gratitude.

26 LOG ENTRY #23

Human beings are a lot like computers. What you put in is what you get out. If you are surrounded by negativity and stress, you aren't going to have a positive outcome. It's impossible to eliminate every bit of negativity in life, so it's almost like damage control. When you surround yourself with negativity and digest it and other stressors, you have no chance against anxiety, depression, and other mental illness.

27 LOG ENTRY #24

THESE WERE REAL FEELINGS I HAD LAST NIGHT....I WAS VERY depressed, negative, and stressed out. The local and national news were on the TV almost all day in my house, and I skipped a meal. Are these feelings valid or was I symptomatic, or both? Here was my social media post from last night.

NOVEMBER 20, 2020

I'm not feeling like my normal happy self. Please pray for me. It doesn't pay to be kind. I've been beaten and tortured and I've taken it with a fucking smile, no less. People treat me like shit and don't respect my work because they know I won't fight back.

28 LOG ENTRY #25

Weird day today. I just can't stay awake. Aside from being sober 99% of the time, my method to stay somewhat stable is my medication and sleep schedule. It's completely out of whack today, but I'm stable and in a good mood. I think I finally hit a wall where I just need to rest. I thought I was going to have some time off, but more books are coming Friday. Oh well, good problem to have, and I have more good days than bad, so I don't think I can ask for more. I treated myself to some really expensive coffee, so I'm just enjoying that and a cold, rainy day in Ohio.

29 POEM ENTRY #3

The smoke and ash
Fill my lungs
And that seems to help for some reason
Until next time.
I'm in a hurry to go nowhere
And I don't know what to do
With my shivering body.
More smoke and ash.
And everyone wants money
But I don't really care
I watch a cloud come from my lips
And fill the air
I hope people hate me for who I am
Because they don't occupy my thoughts
Not even for a minute
I have more important things to do

But for right now, I will eat
And rest again
So I can continue at a later time.

12-2-2020

30 LOG ENTRY #26

This was around 2004. The year I graduated from college. I was working at a pizza place, but I also had a third shift job at a gas station near my apartment. I heard there was a meeting for potential candidates to be manager the next day about a 45 minute drive away. I had made my mind up I was going to be a great manager at this gas station. I had run out of plans, money, and energy for going to graduate school, and I had no idea what to do with a degree in psychology. I worked a full third shift and drove myself to the meeting for potential managers. I had to fight to stay awake both while I was driving and at the meeting. At the meeting, I was standing up straight and drinking coffee to stay awake. I was just determined to be a manager at this gas station. It didn't end up working out, but I put a lot of effort into this idea I had. That's how I've always been. If I believe in something, I give 110% with no regard for my health or psychological well-being.

This is why I display my degree in my bedroom almost 20 years later. The amount of effort I put into getting my degree while fighting a psychotic breakdown is really something to be admired. I'm extremely proud of myself for graduating.

31 LOG ENTRY #27

THE TITLE OF MY PREVIOUS BOOK IS "THE ENTROPY OF BIPOLAR Disorder". An Internet troll accused me of using the word entropy because I was trying to sound smarter than I am. Anyone who has taken a basic science course knows what entropy means. I just always think of it as randomness, like how atoms move around in a cell. I used the word entropy because at first, mental illness symptoms can feel very random, and also my book was just a collection of random thoughts and entries, so I thought the word entropy was appropriate. In one of my previous books, I remember saying to my readers, "Be prepared to feel weird sometimes". The symptoms of mental illness and the subsequent medications are not perfect solutions. The ultimate goal is stability as an overall condition, but it just doesn't always work out that way. I am probably considered stable by my doctor, but I still have to fight through symptoms sometimes. These symptoms can be mental or physical. Eventually, you have a mental list of symptoms that you just get used to. So when you have these familiar symptoms, you don't panic or worry anymore. It's just par for the course. I've learned that my symptoms virtually disappear after a nap, so I know if I can bear it long enough to sleep, I will get relief. (My sleep schedule is also closely related to my medication times, so I know the medication does its job as well.)

32 POEM ENTRY #4

With quivering hands
I jot down a few words
Unwavering strength
And goodness of heart
"I have not yet begun to fight"
Another restless night
But yet I still hope and dream
With optimism and enthusiasm
A life charmed in many ways
I have surpassed my predicted days
I don't have another life left
In my old, cold bones
I don't have the luxury of tomorrow
My joy overpowers the sorrow
Another day in the books
Another notch in my belt
What a wonderful victory it will be.

12-10-20

33 LOG ENTRY #28

I just drove myself to get some gas for my truck. It felt like such an accomplishment, and it is for me. I was just thinking back to how bad I've felt in the past. When I had my psychotic breakdown in 2006, it felt like I was going to die, (although I didn't really know what was going on at the time). Before I knew what a panic attack felt like, it felt like I was going to die when I had one. I was so overweight that I couldn't even stand at the stove and cook myself food. My feet were so swollen that I couldn't wear gym shoes. I have absolutely earned the right to be grateful for all the little things and all the small victories I accomplish, like just driving a short distance to get gas for my truck. Being grateful for otherwise small things to other people not only feels good psychologically, but it's the best solution I could come up with from dealing with extreme symptoms and difficulties. It's not my nature to give up or feel sorry for myself, but I had to discover that on my journey. So many good things in my life would have never happened if I had given up.

34 LOG ENTRY #29

I live for the highs and dread the lows. I'm tired at noon and wide awake at midnight. I have to give myself a pep talk to get out of bed. Intense anger, and then apathy and indifference. Different feelings and emotions at unpredictable, differing times of day. I handle it well with medication and support. Sometimes I can drive a car, and sometimes I can't, and I still haven't figured out what it depends on. It seems like I've tried everything. It's hard for me to imagine life any other way. Still fighting almost 15 years later.

35 LOG ENTRY #30

I'M NOT MONEY MOTIVATED. A COMFORTABLE, TEN YEAR OLD jacket is just as good to me as a brand new one. I don't care about status, and I know that life isn't about acquiring as much "stuff" as possible. The only reason I buy "stuff" is because it brings me joy and happiness, which is way more important to me than the actual "stuff", if that makes sense.

I used to practice my signature/autograph in grade school because I thought I might be a professional baseball player some day. I think a lot of kids probably did that. I never thought I would be signing books. I wouldn't mind being famous for my writing because I've worked so hard and been through so much, but money is low on my list of things that are important to me.

I don't have the luxury of tomorrow. I don't even understand what tomorrow means anymore. I write as much as I can because I don't know if there will be a tomorrow. It's almost an act of desperation that has diminished over time since I was first hospitalized. It's getting better. I think about the future a lot more often than I used to.

36 LOG ENTRY #31

In the morning, sometimes coffee is not enough to wake me up, and other times, I cook a few meals for my family for the week. Maybe bake some cookies or brownies. Some days, it feels like the best day of my life, a gift from above. I have a song or two repeating in my head that's been playing for at least a month. I have to lie down in the dark and play games on my phone or listen to other songs. Maybe roll some cigarettes or look through my sports card collection. I go from being fatigued to wound tight with a lot of energy throughout the day. I try to adjust my work and activities accordingly. At night, I'm so happy to be alone and have a nice bedroom all to myself, and then I feel fear and loneliness that no one is with me. I think of all the people I miss. Then I read or watch a sporting event. Eventually, I drift off to sleep, and it starts all over again. I don't have any regrets, and I don't want to be anyone else. Not even for a day. This is my life, and I'm proud of it. Imperfections, struggles, and all.

37 LOG ENTRY #32

I REMEMBER A LONG TIME AGO GETTING FINISHED WITH WORKING A long day, and that amazing feeling of collapsing on the couch and cracking open a nice cold beer. I still chase that feeling because I don't work a traditional job anymore. The difference between working at a pizza place and helping people with mental health is that now, I have no set hours and my work seems to never be finished. That part about what I do is frustrating, but it's very rewarding. It took me 7 years to get approved for disability, and I am grateful for it, but I also feel like I should work for it somehow. That's just how I was raised. Major credit to my mom for helping me get approved for disability because I wanted to quit trying many times. It was a lot to handle with all the red tape and lawyers and such.

One day, my mom took my entire case files with all my medical records with a picture of me to the disability office. She physically drove herself there, and hand delivered all my information. Shortly after, I was approved. It was a miracle for myself and my family. There were times when I wasn't an author and advocate, and I couldn't do much to work for my disability payments. I am able to put in some very rewarding work now, and I'm not going to stop talking about mental health and trying to help others. The only thing I need to watch out for, which I fail at sometimes, is setting limits to relax to protect my own mental health. I don't have all the answers, but I have some. I am struggling along with my readers and others who need help at the same time.

38 LOG ENTRY #33

I don't know if I will ever get used to being a writer and author. The idea that people are paying hard earned money for my words and experiences is surreal to me. The more surreal part is that none of this was planned. Probably a teachable moment here. I took some writing classes in college, but I was supposed to be a Doctor of Psychology, not a writer. When I was first hospitalized in 2006, I couldn't have even dreamed that my life would turn out this way. I didn't even know if I was going to survive, much less make anything significant out of my future. I have such a grateful attitude now, but it developed. I wasn't born with it. I had to struggle to obtain it. Of course, my nature allows me to feel extremes, and I guess I just feel extremely grateful sometimes, which isn't such a bad thing.

39 LOG ENTRY #34

I want to be like Andy DuFresne played by Tim Robbins in The Shawshank Redemption. The scene I am thinking of is when Andy negotiates with the prison guards to do their taxes in exchange for some cold beers for his friends on a hot day while they are putting hot tar on a roof. I know from my brother that this is a very difficult, hot job. How awesome of a gesture is that? Andy doesn't even drink a beer for himself. He just sits there basking in the glory of generosity and kindness. What a feeling.

40 LOG ENTRY #35

3 THINGS

1. Count your blessings when you feel terrible. This will make you shift your mind to the positive things in your life and help you endure the pain.
2. The world won't treat you better because you're a good person. Accepting this fact will help you deal with unfortunate situations better.
3. Almost always be kind! Not only does it make you feel better emotionally, it makes others feel good, too. Being kind can relieve symptoms of depression and even lower your blood pressure!

41 LOG ENTRY #36

Less news. More positive vibes. What do I know? I just have a degree in psychology and 15 years experience living with anxiety and depression. Wrote 4 books about it. I don't know why this is so hard for people to understand. If you ingest negativity, it's really hard to be happy, healthy, and positive.

42 LOG ENTRY #37

I'VE TRIED TO EXPLAIN THIS BEFORE, BUT I'LL TRY AGAIN. I HAD A very simple task to do. Clean the kitchen. It ended up taking me 5 minutes in the end, but psychologically, it seemed like an impossible task because my symptoms are wearing me out today. MENTAL ILLNESS IS EXHAUSTING. Another classic example is taking a shower and personal hygiene type things. I feel like I conquered a mountain after cleaning the kitchen.

43 LOG ENTRY #38

THIS WAS A SOCIAL MEDIA POST DIRECTED AT MY FRIENDS....

Some of you have seen me at almost every stage of my illness—manic, depressed, anxious, intoxicated, reckless, etc. I wouldn't trade my wild days for anything. I'm glad I lived wildly while I could. Those memories help me get through the hardest of days. We were lucky to have survived, first of all, but we were luckier to have each other and understand friendship love at an early age. It's embarrassing for me for my friends to see me when I'm unwell. It's embarrassing that I can't control my mind and body sometimes. I'm less embarrassed around my family, who have supported me the whole way. I do weird things like having to lay in my bed during gatherings, and I just baked cookies at 2am because I was so hyper. It's nothing super weird, I guess. It's just that I have to filter my energy into something productive rather than vices and self medicating.

44 LOG ENTRY #39

I HAD A WEIRD EXPERIENCE TODAY. I HAVEN'T BEEN SLEEPING well, and I think it finally caught up to me. I was exhausted, and even the smallest task felt overwhelming. I think that's one reason why my illness is a disability. I had to completely pause my life to simply rest. It wouldn't have mattered if I had work to do or something super fun. I had to rest. Disability does not mean inability, however. I do many things well and at a high level. It's just that somewhat frequently, my illness tells me to slow down, whether it be exhaustion or anxiety or a panic attack.

45 LOG ENTRY #40

Maybe I did have a drinking and smoking problem. Maybe I still do. I think about it every day. I also think about the hospital every day almost 15 years later. Maybe I just think too much, and my medication has wired my brain differently. Maybe I changed. If I had a few drinks and a smoke, nothing bad would probably happen. Maybe I don't want to risk the small chance that I have a panic attack or something of that nature. I could get away with it. Everyone who loves me would understand and forgive me. Maybe I'm content with my life now. No additives needed anymore.

46 LOG ENTRY #41

SOCIAL MEDIA CAN BE A VERY VALUABLE RESOURCE FOR MENTAL health. I think it's great when people say, "Hey, I'm depressed. Show me some happy pictures." Or "Hey, I could use some encouragement today." Depression is complicated. Sometimes, it seems like there's nothing I can do to cheer up. We've all seen that depression and mental illness can be so painful that people are desperate to end the pain, and they do so in a variety of ways. I founded and created a support page that has about 900 members from all over the world. I try to make at least one post a day. I've been doing this for about 9 years now. Conversely, social media can be detrimental to mental health, but I wanted to talk about the positives for now. You are not alone. I'm struggling right along with you some days, even though it's been 15 years since I was diagnosed. If you needed a sign to keep fighting, this is it.

47 LOG ENTRY #42

I GUSH ABOUT MY MOM SOMETIMES, AND IF I TALK ABOUT MY DAD, it's usually something weird or annoying. I really do appreciate my dad and all his hard work. He has always been the provider and disciplinarian. Emotions and conversations are not his strengths. I'm developing more patience with my parents. We're almost 2 generations apart, after all. All 3 of us have our own way of doing things. I just don't want to give off the wrong impression about my feelings towards my dad. I love both my parents with my whole heart, and I do my best to make sure they're happy and enjoying their Golden Years.

48 LOG ENTRY #43

I WAS IRRITABLE AT TIMES TODAY, AND I DON'T KNOW IF MY parents even noticed because I try to avoid people as much as possible when I am like that. It's very frustrating because I consider myself a very loving person.

49 LOG ENTRY #44

When I was younger, my dad used to make me breakfast before Mass. That's how it was for a long time. Times were so much simpler. It seems like everyone was happier, too. A part of me misses those days, but I would never go back. On a certain Sunday morning when I was about 15 years old, I refused to get out of bed to go to Mass. I think I was just burned out. I had been going to Mass my whole life, plus Catholic schooling. I'd like to attend Mass one of these days. I am too weak and anxious to go right now. I'm not big on organized religion, but it's comforting to be in a place of prayer.

50 LOG ENTRY #45

In the middle of the global pandemic. January 29,2021....

One positive thing about the pandemic is that the general population is realizing how important mental health is. I wish it didn't have to happen this way, but any publicity is good publicity, as they say. Mental health can affect so many things —sleep disturbances, general mood, drug and alcohol abuse, other risky behavior, impulsive and compulsive behavior, and suicide as a final consequence.

51 LOG ENTRY #46

My life has been a lot like riding a rollercoaster, and I don't necessarily mean in the generic, cliché way of the ups and downs of bipolar disorder and anxiety. When I was younger, I was full of excitement and ambition, like when you are waiting in line for a rollercoaster. Then, I started the ride, and I felt the thrill and terror of the first hill. I think of that as my first psychotic break in 2006. During the ride, eventually, you get tired of being jostled around and just want the ride to stop. You are satisfied with the short amount of excitement, and now you are ready to calm down and talk about how much fun you had. But bipolar disorder and anxiety is a rollercoaster that never really stops. Bipolar disorder is a genetic, lifelong illness. I will die with it, unless there's a cure in the future. Sometimes, I wonder if I would even take the cure if it was available. Bipolar disorder does not define who I am, but it is certainly a part of my personality.

52 POEM ENTRY #5

The phone is ringing off the hook,
The television is spouting the same bad news.
So I step outside to enjoy my coffee and a smoke.
I'm not thinking about much
Except how beautiful the snow is on
Another gray day in Ohio.
The closeness of Spring is keeping me going.
I can't wait to feel the warmth and sunshine.
Better days are coming.

53 LOG ENTRY #47

I've been irritable more than usual the last few weeks, and I don't know if it's from being so isolated or the nature of bipolar disorder, or both. In psychology, the answer is usually both or all of the above. I wonder how much my parents notice since I live with them. All that aside, today has been pretty good. I had some trouble sleeping last night, but I rested a lot today. I have a few offers for people to help me dictate my books into audiobooks. I am very close to reaching a deal with someone, and I'm excited about how that new medium is going to work out. My hopes are always to reach as many people as possible.

54 LOG ENTRY #48

I'M NOT A RELIGIOUS PERSON, AND I RARELY PRAY, BUT I PRAYED today. I hadn't planned on it. It just felt like the right thing to do. It was a prayer of thanks for everything I have, and a prayer of hope for better tomorrows. If only for a few moments, I felt a sense of calm. I would never claim to know if everything's going to be okay, but in those few moments, it felt like it.

55 LOG ENTRY #49

I COMPLETED MY FIRST PODCAST INTERVIEW THE OTHER DAY, RIGHT about this time of day. I didn't tell the host this, but it was exactly when I was due for my 4:30 PM medication. For audio reasons, I couldn't talk on my phone with speaker phone so I had to hold the phone up to my ear. I was pretty wound up because my medicine hadn't started working yet, so I stood almost the whole hour duration of the interview. We spoke about a lot of painful things for me to remember. I know it seems like I talk about everything, but there's some things I don't mention very often, and I would rather forget. When the interview was finished, I felt like I had just been through a boxing match, and I had to lay down. The interview should be available soon, and hopefully I can sell some books and further help more people.

56 LOG ENTRY #50

I have some very fond memories of Dayton, Ohio. I miss my friends I made there. I miss the comforting campus of The University of Dayton. Maybe it was just a better time in my life, although I'm pretty content now. There was a bar called Tailgators near my apartment, where I started to sing karaoke as soon as I was old enough to drink in a bar. I've been singing ever since. I always tell people to sing even if they think they suck at it. It's therapeutic and builds confidence.

57 LOG ENTRY #51

Here are some things I've been thinking about. I'm just going to let it fly. Due to the nature of bipolar disorder, I feel extreme highs and extreme lows. The highs can feel euphoric (amazing) or dysphoric (agitated), and eventually, there is a depressing crash. Every time. I'm laying in bed in a relaxed state thinking about how much I love to watch it snow with a cup of coffee and a smoke. I'm thinking about how lucky I am to be alive. I'm wondering why I'm still here. I've done enough work. I've never done anyone wrong intentionally, and if I have, I think I've made up for it. I'm at peace with my past, and I'm at peace with what I've contributed to society. Mental illness will probably always need advocacy, unless experts start discovering cures. I imagine scientists are more concerned with diseases like cancer. I don't have to worry about necessities or caring for my children. I've always believed that I survived because I had a mission and purpose, so I guess the higher forces aren't finished with me yet. I think what I'm trying to say is that my spirit is at peace for when my work is finished. I'm good. I'm lucky to be alive, and I'm blessed.

58 LOG ENTRY #52

ALMOST EVERY DAY, I PROMOTE MY BOOKS. ONE WAY I DO THIS IS making an ad in author support groups and mental illness groups. I offer my books for free in an email with the hope that people will donate to my Venmo, cash app, etc. Yesterday I made such a post, and almost 700 people responded. I only made $35 in donations. It's just a little frustrating. I've had much better luck on other days. I keep sending emails because I always think of the people who are struggling who might not be able to afford my books or have access. Just because I can't save everyone doesn't mean I shouldn't try.

59 LOG ENTRY #53

I HAVE A NEW PSYCHIATRIST, AND OUR FIRST APPOINTMENT WAS today. He's very professional and thorough. Not very friendly, and he kept interrupting me. Not terrible though. I'm learning that it's easier to write out my thoughts than verbalize them. He's putting me on a new medication called gabapentin. It helps treat chronic pain, anxiety, and seizures. I'm excited to try something new as I have been on the same cocktail for almost 10 years. I figured out that my irritability comes from being in physical pain, so I hope this new medication helps. The other 3 medications I take are Invega, Trileptal, and Klonopin. I ended up discontinuing the Gabapenten because it was making me tired and depressed. I take Naproxen 3 times a day now for pain, and it's working.

60 LOG ENTRY #54

My college experience was different from most students at The University of Dayton. My freshmen year, I lived in the dorms, and I didn't need to have an outside job. Starting sophomore year, I decided to have my own apartment off campus and work full time while attending classes full time. I had an almost around-the-clock schedule until I graduated in 2004. I have always had an uncanny ability to retain information the first time, and it has always served me well. I used to wear my work uniform to class when I did attend class to save time. Many of my professors were lenient with my physical attendance, which I truly appreciate. I don't think I'm smarter or better than anyone else, but I worked my tail off to earn my degree, and I'm a proud graduate.

61 LOG ENTRY #55

One thing I've always found interesting about being diagnosed with a mental illness is the delineation between personality and my disorders. Where does my personality begin and where does my disorder begin? In the end, it doesn't matter because the end result is the person I am. However, there are things I can try to do to help alleviate my symptoms, which may change my personality. They are far from mutually exclusive. Hopefully, that makes sense. Someone who is in pain all the time may not always have a sunny disposition.

I started a medication a few days ago called Gabapenten, also known as Neurotin. Its primary purpose is to relieve nerve pain, but also has qualities of reliving anxiety. I am noticing a small difference in my pain level, which has affected my disposition from irritated frequently to irritated slightly. It's not a perfect solution, and there are no magic pills, but I think I will continue this medication.

I'm a believer in science and mental illness. I've experienced a wide range of symptoms for almost 15 years now.

When I was first diagnosed, I was the most depressed I've ever been in my life. I was a zombie from the sedatives. It was a few years before I could even think about trying to function again. I started by reading inspirational, motivational, spiritual, and philosophical quotes and sayings. I started to feel a little better. I started to gradually incorporate chores and "normal" daily activities into my life. I was even able to return to work full time. I try to keep a positive attitude now above almost anything else. It's important to me. The reason I'm mentioning this is I want to tell people that you may have more choice to be happy than you think. There's an amazing quote that talks about having no chance to be happy if you surround yourself with negativity. It's absolutely true. It's just hard to figure out if it's clinical depression/chemical imbalance, or something that can be solved with positive action.

62 LOG ENTRY #56

I WAS TALKING TO MY MOM ABOUT GETTING OLDER. I'M GOING TO be 40 years old in October, which is shocking to a lot of people besides myself. The neighborhood and friends of my family have watched me grow up. I was telling my mom about the fun my friends and I used to have, mainly at music festivals. Those were some good times. A lot of us were wannabe hippies, but maybe we were all just old souls. By my age, a lot of people have families of their own, and I don't see that happening for me. Times were so much different when I was a teenager. No social media. Not many people had cell phones. You had to buy a disposable camera and have pictures developed. The music scene was some of the best times of my life. When I'm having a rough day, I try to remember all the good times we had, and it helps. Anyway, I hope the next generation still has some old souls and doesn't let the world get to them too much.

63 LOG ENTRY #57

FEBRUARY 23, 2021

IN THE MIDDLE OF A GLOBAL PANDEMIC. APPROXIMATELY 11% OF THE POPULATION IS VACCINATED.

I'VE BEEN FIGHTING THIS BRAIN ILLNESS OFFICIALLY FOR ALMOST 15 years. Even still, I have to go back to the basics of what got me to this point in my recovery. I just had an episode where I was anxious and physically sore to the point where I had to lie down and let my medication work. I managed to shave my face and send some emails. That might be all I can do today, and even now, the day will have been a success. I have to protect and take care of myself even though I'm high functioning. If I forget to take care of myself, my brain and body remind me. I'm hoping I feel better after lunch and a nap. Having symptomatic episodes is always very humbling. And yes, a little discouraging and depressing, but I'm still here fighting and the sun is out. I'm taking a break for a few hours, and hopefully I will have recovered.

64 LOG ENTRY #58

Yesterday was one of the worst days I've had in a very long time. My whole body hurt, including my chest from anxiety, which is very unsettling if you've ever experienced it. I was symptomatic nearly all day, and I went 18 hours without a bite to eat. So much pain. Resiliency matters, and I wish I could bottle it up. I have no idea how I have gotten this far. My mind was racing out of control, and I felt like I might lose my mind. But I didn't, and the sun still rose this morning, just like every day. Almost everyone is experiencing trauma right now and getting a taste of what mental illness and isolation are like. I'm asking you to go to that place in your heart where you usually don't go because it's terrifying, and fight like Hell. We need as many good people in good health as possible right now and in the future. I have to protect my own mental health, but you can reach out to me if you are struggling, and I will do my best to help you. Whatever you do with your life, don't forget love and do it with love.

65 LOG ENTRY #59

I FEEL PRETTY STABLE TODAY FOR THE FIRST TIME IN A FEW DAYS. I think the new medication I tried is out of my system. I had high hopes that Neurotin was going to solve all my problems, so I'm a little disappointed. It was the first new medication for me in about 9 years. I don't really like my new psychiatrist, but we've only had one appointment, and I'm not giving up on him yet.

I think what happened was I got off schedule a few days ago, and I was in physical pain from anxiety. If I get off schedule, my OCD runs wild and causes extreme anxiety to the point of physical pain.

I hate structure, but I need it to stay stable. I take it very seriously. Stable is not fun. Mania is fun. Getting wasted is fun. Even a small deviation can cause all sorts of problems, from mania to depression to anxiety to physical pain. I have to monitor my meal times, how much I eat, medication times, and times when I need to rest. I even monitor how much coffee I drink. It seems like when I'm not as careful about monitoring my illness is when I struggle the most, which seems obvious, but having structure in my life is not enjoyable. I don't feel like a free person sometimes. Not being able to drive when and where I want compounds that.

I was overwhelmed with things I wanted to improve in my life. I had one bad day, and I was questioning everything I've ever done. A spiral (mostly downward) is definitely a good representation of how mental illness can take hold of a person. I'm so worried about improving that I don't stop to enjoy everything I've accomplished.

I used to worry what people will think of me after I leave the Earth, but I'm starting to care less and less. Not because I don't really care, but because I've proven myself, time and time again. If people don't think of me in a positive light by now, I don't know what else I could possibly do.

AFTERWORD

In conclusion, it's important to remember all the great things your brain can do when you are symptomatic, or at least after the symptoms have gone away. I love so many people with a deep love that I don't know if other people feel love so deeply. I'm intelligent. My brain can hold incredible amounts of information, and I like to think of myself as a deep thinker, capable of complex emotions. Unfortunately, overthinking is a by-product of having a complex brain. I've shared my story with everyone who will listen, and I know I have inspired people. Probably saved a few lives. There's no better feeling for me than helping others to that degree. It makes me feel like I have a higher purpose, and maybe my life and my own desires are smaller than the picture I have painted. If you have mental illness, build yourself up every chance you get because mental illness will beat you down. It's not bragging at that point. It's self-preservation.

ALSO BY JOHN MEDL

Millions Like Me: My Struggle with Mental Illness: books2read.com/Millions-Like-Me

Poems From a Bipolar Mind: books2read.com/Poems-Bipolar

The Last Day of July: 13 Years of Madness: books2read.com/Last-Day-July

The Entropy of Bipolar Disorder: books2read.com/Entropy-Bipolar

Mental Illness Is An Actual Illness: books2read.com/Mental-Illness-Actual-Illness

Making Bipolar Lemonade: books2read.com/Bipolar-Lemonade

Bipolar Rising : books2read.com/Bipolar-Rising

ABOUT JOHN MEDL

John Medl is an author with over five published books and a mental health advocate from Cincinnati, Ohio. He has suffered from mental illness for more than eleven years. His diagnoses are: bipolar disorder with psychotic features, obsessive-compulsive disorder, Post-Traumatic Stress Disorder, Generalized Anxiety-Panic Disorder, claustrophobia, and agoraphobia.

John has a Bachelor of Arts in Psychology from the University of Dayton, which he finds ironic.

books2read.com/John-Medl

facebook.com/john.medl
twitter.com/johnmedl7
instagram.com/johnmedl7
amazon.com/author/john-medl

Lightning Source UK Ltd.
Milton Keynes UK
UKHW022136060223
416584UK00025B/558

9 798215 654781